CULTURED

Food Life

DONNA SCHWENK

Learn to make probiotic foods

IN YOUR HOME

www.culturedfoodlife.com

Be Alive Inside!

Donna Schwenk's
Cultured Food
Life

Balboa Press books may be ordered through booksellers or by contacting:

Balboa Press
A Division of Hay House
1663 Liberty Drive
Bloomington, IN 47403
www.balboapress.com
1-(877) 407-4847

Because of the dynamic nature of the Internet, any web addresses or links contained in this book may have changed since publication and may no longer be valid. The views expressed in this work are solely those of the author and do not necessarily reflect the views of the publisher, and the publisher hereby disclaims any responsibility for them.

Edited by: Nancy Westergard, Kayli Westergard
Photos by: Maci Schwenk, Kayli Westergard
Logo and graphics by: Shelley Hanna

Visit online at: www.culturedfoodlife.com and www.blog.culturedfoodlife.com

Certain stock imagery © Thinkstock. Any people depicted in stock imagery provided by Thinkstock are models, and such images are being used for illustrative purposes only.

ISBN: 978-1-4525-3522-7 (sc)

Library of Congress Control Number: 2011909376

Printed in the United States of America

Balboa Press rev. date: 6/10/2011

Dedication

To my daughters Maci and Holli, who came into my life to teach me that wisdom
was just a prayer away, and that we were truly meant to live a life of joy.

To my son DJ, the kindest person I know, and my husband Ron,
who has been the love of my life for 27 years.

It is all of your lives that have caused me to be more than I ever
thought I could be. Thanks for filling my life with love!

Contents

Cultured Food Life:
The Conscious Food You Should Be Eating

Imagine people who have bodies that are so specially designed that they have acquired unbelievable health and longevity. They express incredible joy and well being as they go about their daily lives. They are the type of people that you watch and wonder what is it that they have and what gives them such an advantage. These special people are equipped with hundreds of trillions of cells that are not of human origin. These cells govern everything they digest. They break things down in their bodies and make fatty acids, vitamins and hormones, and then send them on their way to create the wellness that seems to radiate from within. There are so many of these special cells that they would cover the surface area of two tennis courts inside the body, and yet they seem to work in perfect harmony knowing just what to do to create wellness.

These people do exist! In fact, these people are supposed to be you and me. However, few have experienced the joy and well being that our bodies were designed to give us. So I set out many years ago to discover the secret to living in agreement with the way our bodies were designed and how to gain the full benefit of these amazing unseen cells, called bacteria.

The number of bacteria is greater than the number of cells in the body. There are hundreds of trillions of bacteria in the body! Yet they seemed to be ignored except for the times that the harmful bacteria make themselves know through disease. They call out to us when the number of bad bacteria out numbers the good bacteria. Yet in all their attempts to seek balance the body's beneficial bacteria are destroyed and left to fend for themselves. My quest was to discover how to live in harmony with the beneficial bacteria that our bodies need to thrive.

So this is where my story begins; a journey that has filled me with understanding, ancient wisdom, and much joy. **Welcome to your inner world which goes on mostly without your understanding, but longs to work in harmony with you.** Learn as I have to create wellness through special foods that feed this consciousness within, and that governs your beautiful body.

Welcome to the magical world of beneficial bacteria and yeasts; they have been waiting for you.

Finding Your Harbor of Healing

As this journey begins for you, it is my heartfelt desire that I share with you what has been so freely given to me. I am not offering theories, but real stories that include my close friends and real events that are dear to my heart. My hope is that these stories will encourage you on your own healing journey.

Cultured foods have been an incredible gift to me. I am continually amazed how these powerful cultured foods reproduce themselves for a lifetime and cost very little to make. I have also heard and witnessed many stories about cultured foods, and I am always surprised by the diversity of problems they seem to help. I have often said that there is more going on here than I can explain. These alive cultured foods seem to help more problems than I could have ever imagined. As the years pass, the stories of their magic grow. I hope you will learn to love these foods that have meant so much to me. Thanks for reading and I am confident you will find your own harbor of healing.

Meet My Friend, Kefir

I was 41 years old. Although I was holding my new baby in my arms, it was not the beautiful experience I had hoped for. My little one was born 7 weeks prematurely and weighed only four pounds. Her early birth was caused by me. The doctor took her early because I could no longer go on with the pregnancy due to my severe preeclampsia. I was told that my liver was shutting down and she had to be delivered immediately.

I had diabetes that had started during pregnancy, and then went away, only to return a few months later after she was born. I knew a lot about diabetes and as I looked at my beautiful baby in my lap I knew I had to change. I wanted to be vibrant and healthy for this little one that I had to raise. I knew that I could not do this well and have diabetes. Mostly though, I wanted to live and live long. I believe that life is supposed to be one of joy and I was definitely not living that way.

I will never forget that day sitting in the rocking chair with tears rolling down my cheeks. I cried out for help and wisdom from a deep place in my soul. Little did I know that this baby was coming into my life to save me, and to teach me who I really am. Here is what happened:

Holli, my little one, was 10½ months old when she decided to stop nursing. Normally, this would not have been an issue, but for a baby that was born 7 weeks early it was a big problem. Babies receive the mom's immunity in the last 6 weeks in the womb. Babies like Holli who were born 7 weeks early don't get that immune protection. The hospital staff had stressed this point to me when she was born. The only way to protect her was to nurse her as much as possible for at least a year or two. Preemies are more susceptible to all kinds of complications from everyday colds and flu's.

When I started trying formulas and regular cow's milk, she began having frequent colds and many sleepless nights. It was not only hard on her but on me as well. Then one afternoon I stumbled upon a book in a health food store called *The Body Ecology Diet* by Donna Gates. I picked up the book and it fell open to the page on kefir and an explanation of kefir benefits. I was intrigued. Right next to that book was another book called *Nourishing Traditions* by Sally Fallon. When I opened that book I stumbled upon another page on kefir. A store employee walked by as I was holding the *Nourishing Traditions* book. He stopped and turned to me and said, "That is the most important book you will ever read, you should pay attention. It could change everything you thought you knew." Then he just strolled away. I had never heard of kefir and yet in a few minutes two separate books had opened to pages on kefir, and a total stranger had told me to pay attention. Now I was paying attention. I walked over to the store shelf and scoured the shelves for kefir and found a bottle. Putting the kefir and books in my cart, I went home to read about this food called kefir, and quietly hoped that I would find something that would make me and my little one better.

Immediately I began to add 1 to 2 teaspoons of kefir to bottles of raw goat's milk for Holli. What happened next shocked me. In one month my baby gained 4 pounds! That is a lot for a preemie. She had color in her cheeks and she was sleeping at night for the first time. She stopped spitting up everything, and she began thriving. My husband started putting a lot of kefir in her milk and she guzzled it. In a short time, she became the healthiest person in the house.

I started drinking the kefir too. Then not too long after, I remember one day standing at my kitchen window looking out at my birds and thinking, "They are hungry. I am going to run out and give them some bird food." Now you may not think this is a big deal but when you feel sick and run down you don't care at all about the birds. They can feed themselves. Yet now something had lifted inside of me and I felt joy and well being. Feeling joy was how I was supposed to feel and I had forgotten it. My blood pressure was healthy and my blood sugar numbers had normalized. I became addicted to the good feeling and wanted to feel like that every day. This was just the beginning and I was a woman on a mission to discover what had happened to me. What was this kefir and how had it changed Holli and me so dramatically? What was in this ancient food that restored me to my true self?

What is Kefir?

Kefir is a fermented milk drink. The word kefir is said to have originated from the Turkish word "keif" which means "good feeling".

Kefir is an ancient drink. The consistency is creamy and sometimes bubbly. It is similar in appearance to pourable yogurt, but kefir is not yogurt. Homemade kefir has 30 plus good bacteria as compared to yogurt which has only seven. Kefir creates a colony that remains in the digestive system. Yogurt passes through the body within 24 hours, while kefir stays and takes up residence. Yogurt is food for kefir and other dominate bacteria. Kefir kills pathogens and sends them on their way. It then burrows in to the walls of your gut and sends out its little army, like a swat team, to become the dominate bacteria that reduces inflammation and a million other problems. The result of kefir's activity makes you thrive. Kefir acts like a key to a door, unlocking the cells to deliver oxygen for curative benefits as well as nutritional ones. It does all of this hard work while you go about your day.

You can make kefir or buy it pre-made in the stores. *Lifeway* is a brand of kefir that has a variety of wonderful flavors and buying kefir is easier for someone with a busy schedule. I have seen many people gain great benefits from store bought kefir. Make it or buy it; drinking kefir will greatly enhance your life.

Kefir, Blood Pressure, and Diabetes

Many years ago when I was battling high blood pressure and diabetes, I noticed an interesting trend. It seemed that when I drank a glass of kefir every day, my blood pressure would go down. My blood pressure didn't just lower a little bit but significantly enough to put me back into the normal range. When I would stop drinking kefir, my blood pressure would start creeping up within about 3 days. I then started doing experiments on myself to see if it was the kefir that was truly making the difference. After many trial runs, I was convinced it was the kefir. A couple months later my findings were confirmed while reading a book called *Bacteria for Breakfast*. One of the chapters described fermented milk products and their impact on lowering blood pressure for people with mild hypertension. They did a study on rats and humans that confirmed this finding (Yamamoto et al., 1994). Interestingly, some strains of probiotic food produce their own ACE-inhibiting substances during fermentation process. Although most bacteria that produce lactic acid also produce ACE inhibitors during milk fermentation *Lactobacillus helveticus* was identified as the most effective, out of 26 different strains that were tested. However it is important to note that the results were most effective for patients with mild hypertension. The study stated; that it worked on an enzyme in the stomach much like an ACE inhibitor drugs will do. It will naturally lower blood pressure. I am not advising anyone to get off their medication. However, it may be beneficial for you to add some kefir to your diet and then monitor yourself and see if it has the same effect on you.

Kefir also has blood sugar controlling properties. My diabetes quickly went away when I started adding kefir to my diet. It was quite miraculous to me. I also began to notice this phenomenon in others who attended my cultured food classes. I have a good friend who had become diabetic and was having a hard time controlling blood sugar. When she drank a cup or two of kefir, her blood sugar came into the normal range. Kefir is loaded with lactic acid and enzymes that help control blood sugar levels.

Kefir also helps control inflammation in the body and is also a predigested food loaded with enzymes of its own. It is extremely low in sugar, even more so than yogurt. The many bacteria that convert the milk into kefir eat the milk sugars to convert those sugars into the sour kefir that we ingest. Since kefir breaks the milk down to make it easier to digest, the pancreas is relieved and digestion is enhanced.

Here are some of the benefits that I have encountered in myself and others who consume kefir:

- Eliminates constipation
- Reduces or eliminates allergies
- Enhances digestion greatly
- Greatly reduces or eliminates asthma symptoms
- Reduces or eliminates cold & flu illnesses
- Cures acne
- Treats yeast infections
- Cures or reduces hypertension
- Fights off pathogenic microorganisms
- Promotes a natural "feel good" feeling
- Helps to normalize blood sugar
- Effective as a the strongest natural antibiotic without side effects
- Replenishes the body with good bacteria after antibiotic use
- Treats diarrhea
- Helps people who are lactose intolerant
- Promotes deep sleep

How to Make Kefir

There are two ways to make kefir. You can use live kefir grains that reproduce and will last a life time (if you don't kill them with heat or starve them by not feeding them). The alternative is to purchase kefir sold in freeze dried culture packages. Six kefir cultured packages produce 42 gallons of kefir. Instructions for the packaged kefir are inside the package so I will focus on making kefir with the live grains.

To make kefir using the life kefir grains, you can use any kind of milk, low or full fat, raw or pasteurized, cow, goat, almond or coconut milk. The kefir grains eagerly look to transform your milk into something healthy for you. I personally recommend unpasteurized goat's or cow's milk for the maximum benefits.

Kefir grains can be purchased or obtained from a friend who has excess grains. Here are some resources online: http://www.culturesforhealth.com/starter-cultures/kefir-cultures.html or http://www.torontoadvisors.com/

- Place 1-2 tablespoons of kefir grains in a quart glass jar and fill with 1-2 cups of cold milk. Always keep the grains in milk because they need something to eat at all times. Room temperature milk will culture the milk faster but is not necessary. I always use cold milk from the refrigerator. I love things as simple as possible!
- A good rule of thumb for proportions is to use 1 tablespoon of kefir grains per 1 cup of milk.
- Place a lid on the kefir jar. I like the plastic canning jar lids from the Ball company. Put the jar in a spot in your kitchen that is out of the sunlight. Leave the jar on your counter for 24 hours.
- After 24 hours, remove the kefir grains using either a slotted spoon or a strainer.
- You can now drink the strained kefir (without grains) or you can place your strained kefir in a glass jar to refrigerate for later or to start a second ferment (see below).
- Place your kefir grains in new milk and leave for 24 hours to start the process again.

Some people leave the kefir grains in the milk to ferment for several days. Although this method is acceptable, it makes the kefir very sour. Kefir is meant to be enjoyed and the better it tastes the more you will drink it.

Never heat your grains or place them in a hot jar from the dishwasher. Heat and lack of food are the two things that will kill kefir grains.

Storing Your Kefir

If you are away from your grains for more than 1-2 days, you will need to keep your grains alive by refrigeration and giving them enough food to eat. Here is how to do it:

- Place your kefir grains in at least 2 cups of fresh milk. Keep in mind the ratio rule of 1 Tbsp of grains to 1 cup of milk. I like to store 3 Tbsp of grains in more than 3 cups of milk to make sure that they have plenty of food to eat.
- Place this jar of kefir grains and milk in the refrigerator. The grains will stay alive for one week in the refrigerator in this milk. You will repeat this for each week you want to store them.
- If you are going to be gone longer than a week, double the amount of milk with the grains. The kefir eats the lactose (milk sugar) out of the milk and you want to be sure it has plenty to eat. It is a living colony and needs food just as you do.
- The milk you drain from the stored kefir grains is not really kefir. It is too cold to ferment properly in the fridge. I just discard this milk.

How to Second Ferment Your Kefir

I discovered many years ago a way to make kefir not only taste better but also to increase the nutrients in it: second fermenting. It is the only way I make my kefir now because it is so delicious. It is not difficult to second ferment your kefir, and it reduces some of the sour taste. Second fermenting also increases certain B vitamins, like folic acid, and makes the calcium and magnesium more bio available. Bio available means that your body can take in the nutrients and use them immediately. The kefir that has gone through a second ferment is predigested and loaded with powerful enzymes.

Here's how to second ferment your kefir:

- Make the kefir using the instructions above by placing kefir grains in a jar of milk for 24 hours. Take the grains out, and place the strained kefir in a clamp down jar, or another glass jar.
- Using a vegetable peeler, peel several strips of rind from an organic lemon or orange. (Note: If you don't have an organic lemon or orange, you can place your orange or lemon in boiling water for 30 seconds, then rinse in cold water. This helps remove any chemicals.)
- Place the strips of rind in your jar with the kefir and clamp down the lid.
- Leave it on your counter for 12 to 24 hours to ferment again.
- Your second fermented kefir is now ready to enjoy or you can place it in refrigerator for later.

This lemon or orange flavored kefir is so yummy, light and creamy. It has a little more carbonation and the added B vitamins will make you feel great. The taste is worth the extra effort!

I have also second fermented my kefir using the following fun and flavorful combinations:

- Cinnamon stick and orange peel
- Chai Tea Bag (Leave the bag in the kefir for ½ day and it flavors your kefir like Chai)
- A couple of strawberries or any other fruit

When I first discovered kefir, I was shocked at all the benefits. The kefir cultures reproduce themselves to the extent that I always have enough to give away to my friends. These cultures will last a lifetime with proper care and they require almost no effort besides feeding them in a jar of milk on my counter. The kefir that these cultures magically create makes me thrive! So I have been compelled to invent all these recipes using **kefir***. Kefir will be my lifelong friend just as it had been for the people in the Caucasus Mountains who have lived on average to be over 100 years old. They consumed kefir daily and enjoyed great health at a time when there were terrible problems with TB and other diseases. Kefir has done wonders for me that I could not find through supplements or medicine, and has given me a sense of well being that I had never known. How could I not find recipes and ways to promote and enjoy this food? In my small way, I want to give back what was so freely given to me through these cultures that are free and reproduce themselves for a lifetime. It makes my cup runneth over!*

My cup runneth over.

Kefir Smoothies

Smoothies are the most common way to enjoy kefir. I have made hundreds of kefir smoothies. It is also the easiest way to get your kids to enjoy the benefits of kefir.

1 cup of fresh or frozen fruit (Bananas, blueberries, strawberries, peaches, oranges, mangos, etc.)
1 cup plain kefir
Sweetener of choice (Stevia, honey, or sucanat)
½ cup ice (optional, but makes it frothy and bubbly)

Mix all ingredients in a blender at high speed.

Serve immediately.

How to Make Kefir Whey and Kefir Cheese

One of my favorite stories of kefir was from a woman who learned about kefir from my cultured foods class. Several weeks after the class, she emailed me with a miraculous story about how kefir helped her husband. Before kefir, he was unable to eat solid food and had to puree all his meals. He was diagnosed with a rare disease that gave him intense stomach pain unless he pureed all his food. After drinking kefir for a few weeks, he was able to eat solid foods again with no pain!

- Place a basket style coffee filter in a strainer and place the strainer over a bowl. Pour prepared kefir into the coffee strainer. The bowl will catch the liquid whey that will drain through the filter. Cover and place in the fridge overnight. I normally get about 1 cup of whey and 1 cup of kefir cheese out of 2 cups of kefir.
- The next day you have a beautiful lump of kefir cheese in the filter. Remove the cheese from the strainer. You can save the whey that has drained into the bowl for making fermented drinks or cultured vegetables. Store the whey in a glass jar in the fridge.
- You can flavor the kefir cheese with herbs and spices to make a nice cheese spread (see Kefir Garlic Cheese Dip, page 17). You can also use it plain as you would use plain cream cheese.

Kefir draining to make kefir cheese.

Probiotic comes from the Greek words meaning "for life".

Jane's Kefir Cottage Cheese

My farmer's wife, Jane, came up with this recipe and graciously allowed me to use it in this book. It is really quite amazing. Everybody raves about Jane's cottage cheese. When I made it myself I was hooked. You will be hard pressed to find any cottage cheese out there that is better for you. If you knew Jane, you would know why this recipe is so great. She puts her heart in everything she does.

Ingredients:

1 to 2 cups of kefir that has been previously made (the more you use, the quicker it sets up)
1 gallon of raw milk (this will also work with pasteurized milk)

- Place kefir in a gallon of milk in a large pot and bring to 80°F . Then let sit 24 hours or until thickened.
- The next day, bring the pot to 100°F slowly over low heat (about 20 minutes), stirring every few minutes to break up the curds on the bottom of the pan so they won't burn. You will know it's done when the whey separates from the curd. The whey is a clear yellowish liquid.
- Place the whole mixture in a bowl with a strainer that is lined with a cheese cloth. Drain the whey by twisting the bag and the whey will drain through the cheese cloth.
- The finished curds may have consolidated somewhat but are easy to separate.
- You can now add a bit of salt to suit your preference (about ¼ - ½ tsp should do). This is not necessary if you want a salt free product.
- You can also cover with a little cream or milk which makes it quite delicious. Place in the refrigerator in a covered dish to store.

*Our bodies are our gardens –
our wills are our gardeners.*
William Shakespeare

Favorite Preparations of Kefir Cottage Cheese

I make one of these recipes at least 3 times a week. I really enjoy this cottage cheese and top it with a little milk to make it creamy. I also like to eat this with a chopped baked apple on top.

Apple Kefir Cottage Cheese

1 cup Kefir Cottage Cheese
1 apple chopped
Cinnamon sprinkled liberally

¼ cup walnuts chopped
2 packages Stevia or 2 Tbsp honey

Mix all ingredients together.

Blueberry Kefir Cottage Cheese

1 cup kefir cottage cheese
¾ cup of fresh or frozen (thawed) blueberries
1 Tbsp sliced almonds
1 tsp cranberries or 1 tsp goji berries
Cinnamon sprinkled liberally
2 packages Stevia or 2 tbsp honey

Mix all ingredients together.

Tuscany Kefir Cottage Cheese

Fresh basil leaves thinly sliced
Cherry tomatoes
Green onions chopped
Aged Balsamic vinegar, drizzled over the top

Mix all ingredients together.

Strawberry Lemon Basil Kefir Pie

The combination of basil, vanilla and strawberries in this dish is like bringing spring inside. You would think that the basil would be overpowering but instead it tastes both fresh and sweet.

Crust * for a gluten free crust option see below
1 ½ cups of sprouted graham crackers that have been crushed in a food processor (see page 55)
4 Tbsp melted butter

Filling
2 Tbsp unflavored gelatin
¾ cup of milk
2 tsp vanilla extract
5 to 6 basil leaves, chopped
1 cup of 2nd fermented lemon kefir (or plain kefir)
 8 ounces of kefir cheese (you can also use cream cheese)
Zest and juice of one lemon
1 cup of chopped strawberries
4 Tbsp of powdered Stevia (or 4 Tbsp of honey)

For crust: Mix all ingredients in a food processor, about 7 to 8 pulses until well blended. Then press into bottom and sides of an 8 inch pie pan.

Filling: Place milk and gelatin in a pan and heat until gelatin dissolves and mixture comes to a boil. Cool for 5 minutes. Place cream cheese and milk in a food processor with vanilla, basil and lemon zest and juice and process for 30 seconds or until thoroughly mixed. Before you add kefir, make sure that your mixture is cool and not hot. You don't want to kill the good bacteria in the kefir. Add kefir and sweetener to the cream cheese mixture and process until thoroughly mixed – about 15 to 20 seconds. Taste your mixture until sweetened to your taste. Pour into pie pan on top of crust. Chill for about an hour or until firm. Place strawberries on top. Eat and Enjoy!

*Gluten free crust option
1 ½ cups of almond flour or almonds that have been crushed in a food processor.
3 tbsp melted butter
3 -4 chopped dates
Mix all ingredients in a food processor, until well blended. Then press into pan.

"One filled with joy preaches without preaching"
Mother Teresa

Kefir Garlic Cheese Dip

Kefir is my favorite food. Although I love yogurt and I think it is a wonderful food to eat often, I always find myself drawn back to kefir. Kefir has anti-inflammatory properties that eliminate any stiffness in my body. If I stop eating kefir, I get aches in my knee. As soon as I resume consuming kefir, the aches quickly go away. Kefir has many more types of bacteria than yogurt and the kefir colonies significantly increase your body's ability to handle strain, such as joint pain and stiffness.

6 ounces of kefir cheese
3 ounces cream cheese
1 head of garlic
¾ cup grated Romano cheese (or you can substitute Parmesan)
3 tbsp olive oil (If you can find an olive oil with Tuscan flavors such as basil and herbs it makes a wonderful flavor but not necessary)

Wrap whole head of garlic in foil and bake in oven at 375 F for one hour. When the garlic is cooled, squeeze garlic out of each clove. It will be very soft and squeeze right out. Place in a food processor along with other ingredients. Process until smooth, for about 1 minute. Place in bowl and drizzle with a little more olive oil. Serve with crackers or vegetables.

Kefir Croutons

These croutons are super easy to make. They taste buttery and are great on salads. You can also use them to dip in your kefir cheese.

⅔ cup flour
3 Tbsp butter
5 ounces of kefir cheese

In a bowl or food processor, combine all three ingredients and process until smooth. Roll the mixture into logs as thick as quarter coins, or bigger depending on how big you would like your croutons. I like mine big. Chill in wax paper for at least an hour. Cut the logs into coin shapes about ¼ inch thick. Brush with one egg white lightly beaten. Sprinkle lightly with Celtic sea salt.
Bake for 15-20 minutes at 375°F until lightly browned. Cool and serve.

Kefir Ice Cream with Magic Shell Topping

Have you ever had a chocolate dipped ice cream cone? Well now you can have it again! This topping is made with coconut oil which is a staple in our house. When my daughter had terrible yeast and stomach problems, she took coconut oil daily and received great benefits. Coconut oil has caprylic acid, a candida killer. Since coconut oil is a medium chain fatty acid, it is more easily absorbed in the digestive tract and helps other nutrients become absorbed as well. Coconut oil also raises the metabolism and stimulates the thyroid. These benefits are not just words to me, I have witnessed the results.

Kefir Ice Cream
1 ½ cups milk
1 ½ cups plain kefir
1 tsp vanilla
3 egg yolks
½ cup of honey
Place all ingredients in the blender and blend for about 1 minute. Chill in the refrigerator for 20 minutes. Pour into ice cream maker and process with manufacturer's instructions.

Magic Chocolate Topping
½ cup of coconut oil
¾ cup of dark chocolate cut into small pieces

Melt topping in a sauce pan over low heat until chocolate is almost, but not entirely, melted. Let mixture rest for a few minutes off the heat until completely melted. Drizzle mixture slowly over cold ice cream. The coconut oil will harden in a few seconds when it hits the cold ice cream.

Pour any extra melted chocolate mixture into a squeeze bottle or a recycled maple syrup container. The mixture does not need to be refrigerated for storage. It will be liquid at room temperature in the warm summer months, and will be hard during the cold winter months.

"It's supposed to be a secret, but I'll tell you anyway. We doctors do nothing. We only help and encourage the doctor within."
Albert Schweitzer, M.D.

Kefir Coconut Ice Cream with Mango Soup

I love the water; it is the place I feel most at home in the world. When I went to the Caribbean, I thought I had died and gone to heaven. It was the bluest water I had ever seen. The food was just as wonderful. Coconut was in everything, and I love coconut. When I came home I played Jimmy Buffet and made coconut dishes for an entire year. I still use coconut daily. The many virtues of coconut are vast. Unappreciated for many years, it is now fast gaining in popularity. It is a much loved staple in our house and oh, so good for you!

Kefir Coconut Ice Cream
1 can unsweetened coconut milk
½ cup kefir (I use the 2nd fermented orange kefir but you don't have to)
2 -3 packets of Stevia or you can also use 3-4 Tbsp honey
1 tsp vanilla

Blend in blender and place in ice cream maker. It will freeze in about 10 minutes. I love these machines!! Make the soup while the ice cream is freezing.

Mango soup
2 whole mangoes peeled and cubed
1 cup strawberries or 6 large berries chopped
juice of 1 orange

Blend in blender until mixed and creamy. Serve soup with a scoop of kefir coconut ice cream. Garnish with shredded coconut.

Chocolate Kefir Zucchini Cake

Making this cake with sprouted flour is ten times better than using regular flour. But going to the store and buying regular spelt flour and making this cake is still better than buying a cake at the store. Cakes in stores are made with hydrogenated oils and preservatives and chemicals. It is so much better to make it yourself, with or without sprouted flour. There are a ton of nutrients in this cake. And never underestimate the love you put into this cake by trying to make something healthy for your family. Love trumps it all!

½ cup butter
½ cup coconut oil
1 cup Kefir
3 Tbsp Cacao or cocoa powder (Cacao is the raw unprocessed form of chocolate).
2 cups grated zucchini
2 eggs
1 tsp vanilla
1 cup maple syrup
½ tsp salt
1 tsp baking powder
2 ½ cups of spelt sprouted flour

Cream butter and oil together. Add next 6 ingredients, then combine dry ingredients adding a cup at a time and mixing until well combined, about 2 minutes. Pour into a 9x13 greased baking pan and bake for 40 to 45 minutes at 350°F . If you would like to bake it in a Bundt pan, increase baking time by 10 minutes.

Chocolate Kefir Topping
1/4 cup of plain kefir
3 ounces of organic chocolate chips or cacao chocolate chips

Place chocolate in double broiler pan and place on low heat and stir until melted. Remove from heat and when chocolate is warm, but not hot, about 100 degrees or less than add kefir and stir till well combined. Drizzle chocolate kefir over cake.

Apple Kefir Blue Cheese Dip

I started out drinking kefir that I purchased from the store. Then I bought the kefir culture starter packets that make gallons of kefir. Then I purchased living kefir grains and have been making it ever since. I received great benefits from all these methods of consuming kefir. I still buy kefir from the store and use the unique flavors in certain recipes. I also still make it every day from the grains. I am not a person who will say there is only one way to do it. There are so many benefits that I hope that whatever way you decide, to drink or make kefir, that you will make it a part of your life. Find the way that suits you best. Just drink it; the benefits are many.

4 ounces crumbled blue cheese (you can substitute with feta or cheddar)
8 ounces kefir cheese (drained for 24 hours)
3 tbsp dates minced pitted
½ lemon, juiced and zested (less if using feta)
¼ tsp Celtic sea salt
1 cup chopped walnuts or pecans
½ tbsp garlic powder
½ tbsp onion salt
1 small apple chopped into tiny pieces

Garnish: ¼ cup minced fresh parsley
Apple slices for dipping

Mix all ingredients (except parsley and apple slices) in a food processor or by hand. Refrigerate for a 1 hour, and then top with minced parsley. Serve with apple slices or crackers or vegetables.

Apple Kefir Breakfast

In the winter sometimes the last thing you want is a cold smoothie. This recipe is a way to eat your kefir and still feel cozy on a cold morning. It is a great breakfast idea or a wonderful snack or dessert. It is warm and comforting. You can always pour kefir on your oatmeal too for a warm breakfast treat. Best of all, it makes the house smell heavenly. You will be surprised how delicious this tastes!

Serves 2

2 medium sized apples (Golden Delicious or Rome Beauty)
2 Tbsp butter
1 Tbsp sucanat
2 Tbsp chopped walnuts
¼ cup of water

Wash and core the apples almost to the bottom. Don't core all the way to the bottom. Take an apple peeler and peel a thin strip all away around the top of the apple. Place them in a baking dish. Combine the butter, cinnamon/sugar mixture and walnuts. Fill the cavity of each apple with the mixture, dividing it evenly among the two apples. Pour the water into the bottom of the baking dish. Bake at 375°F for 30 minutes. Then let cool and make the kefir topping.

Kefir Topping
2 cups plain kefir
2 tsp cinnamon
4 tbsp maple syrup (or four packages of Stevia for a lower sugar option)

Mix plain kefir with the cinnamon and maple syrup and blend in blender. You can also use stevia in place of the maple syrup if you want to cut down on sugar. When the apple is warm, not hot (you don't want to kill the good bacteria), pour kefir topping over the top of apple and serve. You can add some golden raisins and extra walnuts if you like. This is really delicious !

Kefir Fruit Dip

Did you know that day lilies are edible? The taste is a cross between zucchini and celery; they are delicious. The day lily has a long history in Chinese medicine and cuisine. The Chinese used them as a painkiller. Bach flower remedies, which contain lilies, are used on humans and animals alike. Stuff this fruit dip in day lilies and surprise your guests.

8 ounces of kefir cheese
½ cup chopped pineapple
2 -3 tsp of honey or 2 packets of Stevia

Combine all ingredients, mix well in food processor or by hand. Serve with a large platter of mixed fruit such as strawberries, blueberries, cantaloupe, raspberries, orange slices, etc.

Kefir Blue Cheese Dressing

This is an easy way to get kefir in your daily diet. Pour over a salad wedge and garnish with extra blue cheese crumbles and chopped tomatoes.

Makes 2 cups

Juice of half of a lemon
½ cup mayo
½ cup kefir plain
½ cup Greek yogurt
1 ½ tsp garlic powder
1 ½ tsp onion powder
3 ounces blue cheese crumble

Mix first six ingredients together with a wire whisk. Then stir in the crumbled blue cheese.

Store this in an air tight container in the refrigerator.

Taylor's PB Chocolate Kefir Pie

I was music major in college, so music is very much a part of my life. Somebody is either singing or music is being played in our house continually. I actually wrote this entire cookbook while listening to music. Whenever I get an idea for a recipe, it will come in a wave. Suddenly ideas will start spinning in my head and take form within minutes. Standing in the kitchen on a Sunday afternoon and listening to a Taylor Swift CD was the moment this recipe was created. I made it so fast; I couldn't remember exactly what I did to create it. I had to make it again to retrace my steps. Some days I wish I had been a singer, or at the very least a song writer. The process of creating recipes feels the same to me. I'm putting my thoughts of food to my own music.

Chocolate Pie Crust
1 cup sprouted graham crackers (see page 55)
4 Tbsp butter melted
1 Tbsp cacao or cocoa powder
To make crust: use crushed sprouted graham crackers equaling 1 cup and add cocoa powder or cacao powder. Place in food processor and blend until smooth. Add melted butter to processor and pulse several times until blended well. Place mixture in a 9 inch pie pan, pressing mixture up around sides and bottom until well covered.

Chocolate Ganache
½ cup of cream
3 ounces of organic cacao chocolate chips or dark chocolate chips. (Cacao is the raw unprocessed form of chocolate).
Place cream in pan and heat until bubbles form around edges of pan. Remove from heat and add chips and stir until melted and smooth. Spread over chocolate crust. Refrigerate while making filling.

The Peanut Butter Kefir Filling
1 cup of kefir cheese
1 cup peanut butter
1 tsp vanilla
5 tsp Stevia or 4 Tbsp of honey
1 cup cream whipped
Mix all ingredients except cream in blender and blend until smooth. Fold in whipped cream until blended, being careful not to deflate the cream. Spread over cooled chocolate filling. Cover and place in refrigerator, overnight or until set. Garnish with some extra chocolate chips.

How to make Coconut Kefir

Coconut kefir is made with kefir cultures but instead of placing it in milk you put it in juice from young green coconuts. Coconut kefir is loaded with probiotics, minerals, vitamins, antioxidants, amino acids, and enzymes. It's a wonderful alternative to pop and taste delicious.

Heat 1 quart of young green coconut water to 92°F or skin temperature. You can find coconut water in the Asian sections of your grocery store or health food stores.

Add entire foil package of kefir starter or ¼ cup of kefir whey, and stir to dissolve thoroughly.

Pour into a closable vessel. A clamp down bottle works well. It will now take 4-5 days for the kefir to culture at room temperature. The coconut water will become cloudy as the culture grows and it will become "fizzy". When the culture is done, add a twist of lime a little stevia, ginger or organic sweetener of your choice. It is also great plain. Then sit down and enjoy this delicious probiotic drink. Or refrigerate for later.

Save 6 tablespoons from each batch to inoculate the next quart of coconut water. It will culture faster each time. Many times it will only take a day to culture. You can do this up to 6 times on each package.

Strawberry Coconut Kefir

This drink is so delicious you'll want to drink it every day. It is fizzy and bubbly and full of flavor. It is a great way to get probiotics in your kids because it tastes so good!

8 ounces of coconut kefir that has been cultured
4 or 5 frozen strawberries
Celtic sea salt (optional)
Chilled glasses

To the coconut kefir, add the strawberries and whirl in a blender. Wet the rim of your glass or goblet and place in sea salt to rim the glass. Pour blended drink into chilled glass.

The Wisdom and Magic of Cultured Vegetables

So many people have never heard of cultured vegetables, but many have eaten sauerkraut and pickles which they did not realize was once a cultured food. However, in man's attempt to make foods more convenient and shelf stable, the food industry took this food and changed the way it was made and destroyed the product in the end. Instead of lacto fermenting the product as in years ago, they made it with vinegar and then heated and canned the product. This method destroyed all the naturally occurring good bacteria and enzymes along with the vitamin C.

For thousands of years lacto fermentation was the way people preserved their food. Lacto fermentation happens when the starches and sugars in vegetables and fruit convert to lactic acid by a friendly lactic-acid producing bacteria. Basically you chop up vegetables, add spices and then add good bacteria cultures (cultures are not necessary but helpful) and submerge the entire mixture under water, then wait a few days while they do their magic. You then have one of the most nutritious foods on the planet. These vegetables are then placed in a cold environment such as a refrigerator where they last for at least 9 months. Aging slowly in the fridge, they take on wonderful flavors much like a fine wine does during fermentation. The bacteria eat the sugars in the vegetables and create nutrients that had not been in the vegetables before. It produces enormous amounts of vitamin C and countless other new nutrients and good bacteria. It is super easy and doesn't require boiling, heating, or countless hours spent over a hot stove in the summer canning.

Cultured vegetables have specific bacteria that are unique to them. They are unsurpassed at helping digest proteins and helping the gut repair damage done by processed foods. They are also great at controlling and eliminating a Candida problem. You cannot go wrong by adding these foods to your diet. A tablespoon at a meal is all you need to create a new ecosystem in your gut.

Cultured vegetables are one of my secret weapons. I am crazy for these foods. They are more than food to me. They work like magic. Here is my story of cultured veggies and the miracles they have preformed for me and my family.

It started with my daughter Maci and her terrible IBS (Irritable Bowel Syndrome). Once she started adding about a heaping spoonful of cultured vegetables to every meal, her gut began to heal and her meals were better digested. Cultured vegetables were huge in her recovery, and she eats them every day to this day.

Cultured vegetables also helped me in the springtime when seasonal allergies would hit. The vitamin C and the anti inflammation qualities of these vegetable worked wonders. Since I was in my teens, the springtime was horrible for me. Being allergic to pollen left me in misery for weeks on end. Cultured veggies have now become my constant companion. They greatly, if not almost entirely, eliminate most of my allergy symptoms.

Another story began when many years ago my husband, my daughter Maci and I ate some bad artichoke dip and food poisoning ensued. My son D.J. came home and asked my little girl, Holli where we all were. He then went room to room to find us all in bed very sick. As I lay in bed moaning, I started to get mad and decided that I was not going down without a fight. I dragged myself to the kitchen and ate 2 big spoonfuls of cultured veggies then went back to bed. In about 30 minutes I was up doing dishes. Maci and my husband were almost crying as they asked me how I could walk around and behave normally. It was those veggies! They work like a swat team inside your body fighting off all kinds of virus and bad bacteria.

Did you know they gave these vegetables to the chickens with bird flu the chickens recovered? These veggies are awesome! Anytime anyone has a cold or flu or any kind of virus I am the first to grab a spoonful of these vegetables. They work so fast to destroy the virus and bring you back to health that it constantly amazes me. The juice is every bit as powerful as the vegetables. Billions of bacteria in these foods will find their way to dominate and destroy many kinds of foreign invaders. It is quite a thing to witness that something as little as a couple tablespoons of a food two or three times can do such much. I love these little microbes unseen by the human eye. I may not be able to see them but they let me know that they are there working on my behalf, and I am most grateful to have them on my side.

So what about botulism and cultured vegetables?

The competing microbial suppresses botulism bacteria making it impossible to take place. When you kill bacteria with heat the only microbes that can survive is botulism. With canning we place these spores in an anaerobic environment where it can thrive. With culturing foods the healthy bacteria make it impossible for this to take place. Acidifying bacteria grow when vegetables are submerged under water and thereby making it impossible for food poisoning to occur.

The Trilogy

Something I have observed over the last 9 years is that wonderful things seem to occur when people include the trilogy of cultured foods. It happened in my life and family first. We would get better as we consumed one of these cultured foods: kefir, kombucha or cultured vegetables. When we added all three to our daily lives our health sky rocketed. Then I began to notice the phenomenon in others. They received great benefit from one of these foods, but when they added all of them it seemed to eliminate all the problems they had been facing. Is it the types of bacteria and good yeasts combined that makes the difference? I believe that this is one of the keys. With all the different types of bacteria presenting differently in these foods, consuming all of them appears to work wonders. After all we have hundreds of bacteria in our bodies. They are smarter than we know and they work to keep us well. This always makes me smile.

Cultured vegetables you can buy

If you don't have time to make these foods you can always buy them. One of my favorites is the Bubbies brand dill pickles and sauerkraut. They are one of the few lacto fermented vegetables on the market, and you will find them in the refrigerator section at your health food store. These products are so delicious that they are easily added to your diet. With billions of good bacteria per serving, you should stock them and always have them on hand. Remember Bubbie's fermented juice is just as powerful as the food itself.

"Cultured foods speak for themselves;
I am just the messenger."

Donnas' Dills

So many of my friends initially thought I was crazy when I would tell them about what cultured vegetables would do. But eventually, one by one, they would all eventually cave in and try these foods. It was usually because of a sick child that caused them in desperation to try something new. These little power house vegetables would convince them that they indeed were more than the normal foods on the market. They would become converts and start stocking them. I would always smile, as they would tell me how they thought I was crazy, until they tried them. Cultured foods speak for themselves; I am just the messenger.

Makes 1 gallon

3-4 lbs of cucumbers (small to medium is ideal, but if all you have is large, cut them into spears)
6 Tbsp Celtic sea salt
3 cloves of garlic
3 Tbsp whole dill seed
2 Tbsp whole coriander seed
1 tsp whole mixed peppercorns
1 tsp juniper berries
½ tsp red pepper flakes
1 tsp fennel seeds
1 veggie culture packet or 1 /2 cup kefir whey
Filtered water

If using a veggie starter, add ½ cup of water then add veggie culture. Feed it a little sugar to wake it up (about 1 tsp) and stir until dissolved. The sugar will be consumed quickly by the bacteria cultures, and there is no need to worry about the added sugar. If using kefir whey, proceed with other instructions below.

Chop cucumbers in half and place flat side down on surface and cut into spears. Place cucumbers in four quart jars. Place other ingredients in a measuring cup with a spout for easy pouring. Mix all ingredients until well combined. Pour mixture into jars making sure that each jar gets an equal amount of ingredients (some of the seed may fall to the bottom).

Fill the jars with extra water leaving a 1 ½ inches of room at the top and making sure veggies are below the water. The veggies will mold if left above the water. If this happens scrape off the mold or discard the top veggies and push the others below the water. The mold is harmless and won't hurt anything but they can ruin the taste of the veggies. Set at room temperature for 3 days and then place in the refrigerator. They taste the best after 3 to 4 weeks in the refrigerator.

Sweet Fermented Pickle Relish

You can also make these into bread and butter chip pickles. Simply leave the cucumbers and onions in thin slices instead of chopping and dicing. These are really good on sandwiches.

Makes 1 quart

3 cups chopped and diced cucumbers
½ cup chopped and diced sliced onions
¼ cup whey or ½ tsp from cultured veggie packet
½ cup honey or maple syrup
½ red pepper chopped and diced
1 ½ Tbsp Celtic sea salt
1 Tbsp whole celery seeds
1 tsp turmeric
½ Tbsp yellow mustard seeds

In large bowl, mix cucumbers with onion and place in a quart-sized, wide-mouthed mason jar, pressing down lightly with a pounder or meat hammer. Combine remaining ingredients and pour over cucumbers, adding more water if necessary to cover. Keep the top of the liquid 1 inch below the top of the jar. Cover tightly and keep at room temperature for about 3 days before transferring to the refrigerator. These will last at least a year in your fridge

Sauerkraut

This recipe does not use kefir whey or a culture package. Cultures are not necessary to make sauerkraut, but I have always found them to be more beneficial in adding extra bacteria and also in creating a consistent finished product. This is an easy recipe; one I have made many times. It is a great place to start when making culture foods for the first time.

Makes 3 quarts

1 head of cabbage
2 tbsp Celtic sea salt

Remove outer leaves of cabbage. Shred cabbage into desired length. You can use a food processor or shred by hand. Pack cabbage into a gallon jug with a clamp down lid. Cover with water. Add salt if you want it crunchy. If you want it softer, leave the salt out. Leave 2 to 3 inches for kraut to expand. Set in a cool place, out of sunlight, for 6 days. It will expanded and bubble which is a result of the fermentation and the developing lactic acid. You can really add any kind of vegetables you want. Check it over the 6 days and push down the vegetables if they come up above the water. When exposed to air, the cabbage will mold over time. It doesn't ruin the whole batch if you find mold on the top; just scoop out the vegetables that are above the water and push the other ones down below the water.

Golden Beet Sauerkraut

This is one of the first recipes I made that my daughter liked. Golden beets have such a unique flavor.

Makes 1 gallon

3 to 4 golden beets (I love these; they taste like sunshine)
1 head of cabbage, purple or green
½ apple
1 inch ginger peeled
Veggie culture starter, or ¼ cup of kefir whey
Filtered water

Place veggie starter culture in a glass cup or jar. Feed it a little sugar to wake it up (about 1 tsp), and then add ½ cup of water stir until dissolved. Then let it sit will you chop your vegetables. The sugar will be consumed quickly by the bacteria cultures, and there is no need to worry about added sugar.

If using kefir whey add it when it calls for culture below.

Peel and shred all vegetables and place in jars or containers. Fill jar with water, leaving a two inch header at the top. Your vegetables will bubble and expand. Let vegetables sit for 6 days out of the sun. Then place in refrigerator where they will last at least 9 months. If the vegetables climb up above the water they will mold. The mold is harmless. You scrape off the mold and submerge vegetables under water. Check from time to time to while they are fermenting to make sure they stay submerged under the water.

Maci's Cultured Carrots

This is one of the first recipes my daughter Maci made herself. She is a great lover of cultured foods and her enthusiasm for them is contagious.

Makes 2 quarts

3 golden beets
1 large Daikon radish
8 large carrots
3 Tbsp of chopped basil or cilantro
Veggie-culture starter or ¼ cup kefir whey

Place veggie starter culture in a glass cup or jar with ½ cup water. Feed it a little sugar to wake it up (about 1 tsp), stir until dissolved. If using kefir whey add it when it calls for culture below.

Peel and shred all items and place in jars. Fill with water leaving a 1 ½ inch cap header at the top for vegetables to bubble and ferment. Let sit for 6 days then place in refrigerator.

Dilly Purple Cabbage

Cultured foods are more than just a good idea or a healthy food. They are literally what you and I are made of. Have you ever thought about what goes on inside you to create the millions of processes that govern your body? Well, the wonderful thing is that you don't have to, because we were created to have these things function automatically.

Beneficial bacteria in the body train the immune system to prevent the growth of harmful, pathogenic bacteria. The human body does not make vitamin K by itself. Beneficial bacteria create this and other essential vitamins and hormones. They also help our bodies to break down drugs and carcinogens, which can cause cancer.

Makes 1 gallon

1 small head of purple cabbage
3 carrots
3 cloves of garlic
juice of 3 lemons
3 tbsp dill weed
1 small beet
Veggie starter culture or ¼ cup of kefir whey
Filtered water

Place veggie starter culture in a glass cup or jar. Feed it a little sugar to wake it up (about 1 tsp), and then add 1/2 cup of water stir until dissolved. Then let it sit while you chop your vegetables. The sugar will be consumed quickly by the bacteria cultures, and there is no need to worry about added sugar. If using kefir whey add it when it calls for culture below.

Peel and shred all vegetables and place in jar or container that will give you at least 2 inches of room at the top to let your vegetables ferment and expand. Place all your vegetables in a food processor or blender and puree. Add some water so it is easier to blend. Add your cultures, leaving a two inch header at the top. Your vegetables will bubble and expand. Let vegetables sit for 6 days on your counter, out of the sun. Then place in refrigerator where they will last at least 9 months. If the vegetables climb up above the water they will mold. The mold is harmless. You scrape off the vegetables with molds and submerge the vegetables under water again. Check from time to time to while they are fermenting to make sure they stay submerged under the water.

Lemon Poppy Seed Veggies

This is everybody's favorite at my house from my little 10 year old to my husband and adult son. They are super picky eaters but this is one recipe they will eat because they like it. It is also really pretty.

Makes 2 quarts

½ head of cabbage
1 large golden beet the size of a large potato
½ tbsp poppy seeds
Juice of 3 small lemons
4 cloves of garlic
½ Tbs of dill seed
Water to puree
Veggie culture starter or ¼ cup kefir whey

Place veggie starter culture in a glass cup or jar. Feed it a little sugar to wake it up (about 1 tsp), and then add ½ cup of water stir until dissolved. Then let it sit will you chop your vegetables. The sugar will be consumed quickly by the bacteria cultures, and there is no need to worry about added sugar. If using kefir whey add it when it calls for culture below.

Peel and shred all vegetables. Add water and place in blender or food processor and puree until smooth and uniform in size. Add culture and place in jar or container that will give you at least 2 inches of room at the top to let your vegetables ferment and expand. Cap and place in refrigerator. This will last at least 9 months in the refrigerator.

Jicama with Orange

This is my favorite cultured veggie. Sweet, sour and salty, it has its own unique taste.

Makes 1 quart

2 small Jicamas, peeled and sliced on a mandolin or in thin slices
2 tsp salt
1 small orange zested and juiced
¼ cup kefir whey or ¼ veggie culture starter package
½ cup of filtered water

Place veggie starter culture in a glass cup or jar. Feed it a little sugar to wake it up (about 1 tsp), and then add ½ cup of water stir until dissolved. Then let it sit while you chop your vegetables. The sugar will be consumed quickly by the bacteria cultures, and there is no need to worry about added sugar. If using kefir whey add it when it calls for culture below.

Add jicama and orange juice, zest and salt¸ then add cultures and water to fill jars leaving a 1 ½ inch header at the top for vegetables to bubble and ferment. Let sit on counter to ferment for 3 days, and then place in refrigerator, for as long as 9 months.

Purple Cultured Onions

Makes 1 quart

2 Tbsp coriander seed
1 Tbsp mustard seed
3 medium red onions, julienned
2 Tbsp sugar
1 tsp salt
1 sprig of thyme
¼ cup kefir whey or ¼ cultured package
½ cup of filtered water
More filtered water to fill jar

"Fermentation is the process of specific bacteria and yeasts that have acquired wisdom beyond our own, therefore transforming our foods into nutrients with added beneficial properties that in turn transform us."

Donna, Cultured Food Life

Place veggie starter culture in a glass cup or jar. Feed it a little sugar to wake it up (about 1 tsp), and then add ½ cup of water stir until dissolved. Then let it sit will you chop your vegetables. The sugar will be consumed quickly by the bacteria cultures, and there is no need to worry about added sugar.

If using kefir whey add it when it calls for culture below.

Place vegetables and herbs in jars press and pack down onions, and then add water and culture to fill jars, leaving a 2 to 3 inch header at the top for vegetables to bubble and ferment.

Let sit on counter to ferment for 5 days, and then place in refrigerator, for as long as 9 months.

Rosemary Fennel

This is delicious as a side dish, especially served with fish.

Makes 1 pint

1 small fennel chopped and thinly sliced
½ lemon, zested and juiced
½ sprig of rosemary
1 tsp salt
1 clove garlic
⅛ cup kefir whey or ⅛ cultured package
½ cup of filtered water

Place veggie starter culture in a glass cup or jar. Feed it a little sugar to wake it up (about 1 tsp), and then add ½ cup of water stir until dissolved. Then let it sit will you chop your vegetables. The sugar will be consumed quickly by the bacteria cultures, and there is no need to worry about added sugar.

If using kefir whey add it when it calls for culture below.

Add fennel and rosemary, lemon zest, juice, garlic and salt, then add water and culture to fill jars leaving a 2 inch header at the top for vegetables to bubble and ferment. Let sit on counter to ferment for 3 days, and then place in refrigerator for as long as 9 months.

Rainbow Carrots & Daikon Sticks

The first time I tried these carrots and daikons I was shocked how something so simple could be so good. The veggies are cut into little bite size sticks and then fermented. It's a little sweet and a little sour. Perfect for kids but craved by adults. You are going to love these. They stay crunchy and crisp.

Makes 1 quart

6 or 7 rainbow or regular carrots cut into match size sticks or Daikon cut into match sticks
½ lemon juiced
¼ cup kefir whey or ¼ cultured veggie package
½ cup of filtered water

Place ½ cup of water in a quart jar with cultured package or kefir whey stir to mix thoroughly. Add carrots, lemon zest, and juice, then add water to fill jars leaving a 2 inch header at the top for vegetables to bubble and ferment. Let sit on counter to ferment for 3 days, and then place in refrigerator for as long as 9 months.

CKC ~ Cultured Kombucha Coleslaw

This is a great coleslaw recipe. Nobody will even know that it is full of probiotics. I love taking this to a get together. This is kind of my way of spreading good bacteria all over my city, the greater Kansas City area.

1 medium head of cabbage, shredded
½ cup cultured carrots, no juice
1 cup mayonnaise
⅛ cup plain kefir
3 tbsp Dijon mustard
½ cup kombucha
1 tsp salt
½ tsp white pepper
½ cup honey

Mix vegetables in a bowl. Mix remaining ingredients in another. Mix together and toss well. Serve or refrigerate.

Rainbow Swiss Chard Stalks

Cut these stalks up and place in a chicken or potato salad. They taste a lot like mild celery.

Makes 1 quart

1 large bunch of Rainbow Swiss chard, leaves removed
with just stalks remaining
1 tsp salt
½ tsp coriander seeds
¼ cup kefir whey or ¼ cultured package
½ cup of filtered water

Place veggie starter culture in a glass cup or jar. Feed it a little sugar to wake it up (about 1 tsp), and then add ½ cup of water stir until dissolved. Then let it sit will you chop your vegetables. The sugar will be consumed quickly by the bacteria cultures, and there is no need to worry about added sugar. If using kefir whey add it when it calls for culture below.

Add, chard stalks, and salt then add water to fill jars leaving a 2 to 3 inch header at the top for vegetables to bubble and ferment. Let sit on counter to ferment for 3 days, and then place in refrigerator for as long as 9 months.

Shelley's Cultured Veggies

This recipe was given to me by a woman who came to one of my classes. She has now become a dear friend and she also did the beautiful graphics for my book. These veggies are so delicious; I ate half a jar the first time I tried them. Thanks, Shelley, you're the best!

1 head of green cabbage (pull off plenty of large outer leaves to use for packing jars)
6 carrots
6 kale leaves or spinach leaves chopped
½ white onion
½ green apple
1 clove garlic minced (add more if you like garlic)
2 Tbsp parsley flakes or chopped fresh parsley
2+ Tbsp or to taste Bragg Organic Sea Kelp Delight Seasoning
2 tsp (or to taste) Celtic Sea Salt (makes veggies more crunchy)
1 to 2 cups filtered or purified water
1 package culture starter or ¼ cup kefir whey

Place veggie starter culture in a glass cup or jar. Feed it a little sugar to wake it up (about 1 tsp), and then add ½ cup of water stir until dissolved. Then let it sit will you chop your vegetables. The sugar will be consumed quickly by the bacteria cultures, and there is no need to worry about added sugar.

With a food processor, shred the cabbage, carrots, onion, and green apple and assemble into a large bowl (you may need a couple of bowls depending on how large of a batch you are making). If you don't have a food processor, you can shred veggies with a large knife or grater.

Mix in the chopped kale, minced garlic, parsley, Bragg Sea Kelp Seasoning and salt. Add optional ingredients as well.

Once veggies are mixed thoroughly, remove a few handfuls (or cups) and put in a blender adding enough filtered or purified water to create a thick brine. You can add in your prepared culture starter at this point and blend well into the brine.

Add brine back into veggies and mix thoroughly.

Pack veggies into glass mason jars mashing mixture down into the jar with your hands, a wooden spoon or a potato masher until juice rises up. Make sure the veggies are packed tightly leaving two inches at the top for expansion.

Roll up outer cabbage leaves tightly and place in the top of the jar to keep veggies under juice while fermenting. Cover tightly with jar lid and leave to ferment on countertop for 3 to 7 days depending on room temperature (ideal is at 70°F for 7 days) Veggies will be a bit fizzy and sour when ready. Place in refrigerator to slow down fermentation process. They will last at least 9 months.

Kimchi

"Let food be thy medicine and medicine be thy food".
~ Hippocrates

Makes 2 quarts

1 head Napa cabbage, cored and shredded
1 bunch of green onions, chopped
1 cup carrots, grated
½ cup daikon radish, grated
1 Tbsp fresh grated ginger
3 cloves garlic, peeled and minced
½ tsp dried chili flakes
1 Tbsp sea salt
½ cup kefir whey or ½ veggie cultured package

Place veggie starter culture in a glass cup or jar. Feed it a little sugar to wake it up (about 1 tsp), and then add ½ cup of water stir until dissolved. Then let it sit will you chop your vegetables. The sugar will be consumed quickly by the bacteria cultures, and there is no need to worry about added sugar. If using kefir whey add it when it calls for culture below.

Place vegetables, ginger, red chili flakes, salt and whey in a bowl. Place them in two quart sized glass jars and press down firmly until all the juices come up to the top and cover the vegetables. The top of the vegetables should be at least an inch from the top of the jar. Cover tightly and keep at room temperature for about 3 days at which time you can put it in the fridge or cold storage.

Tortillas with Culture

These are a quick and easy lunch and something that can give you your probiotics for the day.

⅓ cup kefir cheese
1 clove garlic minced
2 basil leaves chopped or 1 tsp dried basil
4 matchstick cultured carrots cup into tiny pieces
1 cultured dill pickle spear chopped
2 turkey slices chopped
½ cup Monterey jack cheddar cheese shredded
2 spouted tortillas (see page 55)

Mix kefir cheese with minced garlic and basil. Spread mixture on tortillas. Add rest of ingredients into tortillas. Roll up and enjoy.

Cultured Border Salsa

The first time I made these salsas, I completed the task and quickly cleaned the kitchen and jumped into the shower. I never realized that the pepper seed juice that I had on my hands cannot be washed off with soap and water. Needless to say, I started to burn in the shower in places that best are described as delicate. Then finally I realized that soap was not going to take the burning and stinging away. I jumped out of the shower, grabbed a towel, and ran to the kitchen dripping wet and praying that nobody would see me. I opened my refrigerator and tried to pour a cup of kefir into a bowl while clinging to my towel with one hand. I then tried to sneak back to the shower to neutralize the infected areas with a neutralizing agent, my kefir. I finally admitted to my husband what I had done. He replied, "Now that's something I would have paid money to see!" If nothing else, it was a reminder that I probably should have taken some cooking classes in my life. They would have at least warned me of such hazards of cooking. Just please wear your gloves when seeding a pepper or you may just light up your life in more ways than one.

Makes 1 quart

2 large tomatoes, coarsely chopped
1 Serrano pepper, seeded and coarsely chopped
2 tsp cumin
2 cloves garlic, minced
½ large Vidalia onion, coarsely chopped
¼ tsp salt, to taste
⅓ cup cilantro, coarsely chopped
⅛ tsp cayenne, to taste (only if you like it hot)
¼ cultured veggie packet or 3 Tbsp kefir whey

Place veggie starter culture in a glass cup or jar with ½ cup water. Feed it a little sugar to wake it up (about 1 tsp), stir until dissolved. If using kefir whey add it when it calls for culture below.

Place all ingredients in blender, and blend until smooth. Add culture and place in glass jars and seal. Sit on counter for 2 days and then transfer to refrigerator. This will last at least 3 months in refrigerator.

Probiotic Guacamole

This guacamole will last much longer than other guacamoles without turning brown because of the good bacteria and enzymes. So if these cultures help prolong the color and life of the food, doesn't it make sense that it will also do the same inside of you?

3 Avocados
Juice of ½ lime
½ Tbsp Celtic sea salt
3 Tbsp cilantro
1 small Serrano chili chopped and seeded
1 Tbsp lemon poppy seed cultured
1 small onion chopped
4 cherry tomatoes chopped

Scoop out avocados and mash with a fork. Add other ingredients and mix well.

Cultured Bean Dip

I made this recipe for the super bowl this year. My son ate so much I started counting in my head all the good bacteria he had just eaten. I am probably the only person I know who lies in bed at night and tries to remember the names of all the bacteria and yeast in kefir. It is an occupation and habit and I just can't help myself. I love these little microbes that are unseen by the human eye.

1 ½ cups of refried pinto beans
1 cup Cultured Border Salsa
1 cup kefir cheese
2 Tbsp taco seasoning (homemade is best)
Shredded Monterey jack cheese
Chopped black olives
Chopped green onions
Corn chips (preferably organic)
1/3 cup of sliced Jalapenos

Place refried beans in an 8X8 glass pan. Mix kefir cheese with 2 tbsp taco seasoning. Spread the kefir cheese on top of the beans. Spread the salsa on top of the kefir cheese and top that with shredded cheese. Then add chopped black olives and green onions. You can add a layer of guacamole in between the beans and cheese for another added bang! Serve with corn chips.

Fermented Cherry Tomatoes That Pop

These tomatoes are bubbly and fizzy and super good. I have to admit that I love the fizz in fermented foods. It is naturally occurring and not the result of a machine that forcefully adds carbonation.

Makes 1 quart

Enough Cherry tomatoes to fill a quart jar ¾ full
½ tsp of Cultured Veggie packet or 3 Tbsp kefir whey
Filtered water

Wash tomatoes and place in clean sterilized jar. Fill with filtered water ¾ of the way full. Sprinkle a small amount from cultured veggie package into jar, about ½ tsp or add kefir whey. Seal and let sit on counter for 4 days. Then place in refrigerator and ferment about 1 week or longer. They will last at least a year.

Panzanella Salad

The color of all the veggies makes this a beautiful salad. I have heard people gasp when I've served it.

Serves 12

6 cups cubed Sourdough bread or (stale bread works well too)
1 jar of fermented cherry tomatoes
1 medium red onion, halved and thinly sliced
2 medium yellow peppers, seeded and cubed
1 large seedless cucumber, quartered lengthwise, cut into 1" pieces
⅓ cup chopped parsley
⅓ cup extra-virgin olive oil
¼ cup of kombucha
2 teaspoons minced garlic
2 Tbsp juice from fermented cherry Tomatoes
1 tsp salt
½ tsp freshly ground pepper

Heat oven to 400° F. Arrange bread cubes in a single-layer on pan. Toast in oven 10 to 12 minutes, until evenly browned. Meanwhile, combine oil, kombucha, garlic, fermented juice, salt, and pepper in a large bowl. Whisk together. Add tomatoes, peppers, onions, cucumber and parsley to large bowl. Stir in dressing. Just before serving, add bread cubes, toss to blend thoroughly.

Spicy Mustard

This is super spicy before it ferments but mellows after a few days of fermenting.

1 ½ cups ground mustard
¾ cup filtered water
2 tsp kefir whey or ⅛ tsp of veggie culture packet
2 tsp Celtic sea salt
Juice of one lemon
1 clove of garlic mashed (optional)
¼ tsp paprika
2 tbsp honey (optional)

Mix all ingredients until well blended adding more water if necessary. Place in 2 pint size jars and cap tightly. Let this sit at room temperature for 3 days, then transfer to refrigerator.

Ketchup

The ketchup is super easy and is also filled with probiotics!

3 cups of tomato paste, preferably organic
¼ cup of kefir whey or ⅛ tsp of veggie culture packet, plus ¼ cup water
1 Tbsp Celtic sea salt
½ cup maple syrup
¼ tsp cayenne pepper
½ tsp cumin
¼ tsp cinnamon
3 cloves of garlic peeled and mashed
½ cup of fish sauce

Mix all ingredients and place in quart or pint size jars. The top should be 1 inch below the top of the jar. Leave at room temperature for 2 days, than transfer to fridge.

"Disease is the warning, and therefore the friend – not the enemy – of mankind.

Dr. George S. Weger

Make Your Own Apple Cider Vinegar

You will be surprised how delicious homemade vinegar is. I had a friend who tried my vinegar one time and said that she would dream about it and had to have some because it was occupying too many of her thoughts. It really is quite delicious and worth the effort to make it.

1-½ cups of Bragg's apple cider vinegar (with the "mother" in it)
4 ½ cups of good apple cider

Place the vinegar and the apple cider in a crock or jar make sure the crock does not have lead based paint and is food grade. It should hold at least a gallon with enough extra room for air circulation.

Cover the opening with a cloth or cotton tea towel. Place in a warm spot (68 to 70 F) for 1 to 2 months. Check it occasionally and sniff it. It will gradually take on a distinct vinegar smell and you will notice a slight film on the top.

When the mixture taste and smells like vinegar pour a third and place it in airtight bottles. Save the culture and extra vinegar and replace with equal amounts of apple cider and start the process again. The process will take less time so check it often. Mine has been done as soon as two weeks. You can also bottle all of it and throw away the culture.

Red Wine Vinegar or White Wine Vinegar

You can also make red wine vinegar or white wine vinegar using the same recipe but you have to find red and white wine vinegar with the mother in it. This means unpasteurized vinegar. You will see sediment at the bottom of the bottle. It will say "unpasteurized" or "with the mother" on the bottle. I have found some at the local health food store.

1 ½ cups of red wine vinegar with mother (I use the Eden brand with the mother)
4 ½ cups of red wine

Or for white wine vinegar
1 ½ cups of white wine vinegar with the mother
4 ½ cups of white wine

Follow the instructions above.

Kombucha: a Magical Tea

When I first read about kombucha, I was amazed at some of the stories. There seemed to be entire communities of people who not only drank this surprisingly healthy drink, but loved it deeply. There were many who drank it for its prevention and curative effect but then became intensely loyal and devoted. The stories were many and it wasn't long until I too had my own story. I was shocked at how much love I could feel for a beverage! It was kombucha that made me realize that the foods we eat and drink are some of the most spiritual things of all. They change you from the inside out. Kombucha made me feel so good that I could not help but feel more kindness and love towards others. Food talks to your genes and becomes you. It is the very essence of the cells you are made of. There are enormous amounts of B vitamins in kombucha. These special B vitamins lift our spirits and cause us to feel the way we are suppose to feel, alive and vibrant. So if we are what we eat, I am a bubbly combination of yeast and bacteria that is alive and constantly rejuvenating. Yes, I am proud to tell you about my friend, kombucha. I hope you love it too. It makes my heart sing every day.

So what exactly is kombucha? It's pronounced [Kom-boo-cha]. Kombucha is a living health drink made by fermenting tea and sugar along with a kombucha culture. It has been around for hundreds of years. If you are concerned that it is made with sugar you needn't be. The sugar is consumed by the culture leaving you a delicious tart drink. The result can taste like something between sparkling apple cider and champagne, depending on what kind of tea you use. It's not what you'd imagine fermented tea to taste like. It is made and drunk around the world. It has been a "secret formula" for those in the know and a lifesaver for many a poor person in the less blessed nations. I am so impressed with this drink that I have it daily. One of the main reasons I drink Kombucha is for the glucuronic acid, the body's most important detoxifier. When toxins enter the liver, this acid binds them to it and flushes them out through the kidneys. Once bound by glucuronic acid, toxins cannot escape. Glucuronic acid is one of the more significant constituents of kombucha. As a detoxifying agent, it is one of the few agents that can cope with pollution from the products of the petroleum industry, including all the plastics, herbicides, pesticides and resins and heavy metals. It kidnaps the phenols in the liver, which are then eliminated easily by the kidneys. It is such a strong detoxifier that I have come to rely on it for helping with issues of weight loss, allergies, building the immune systems, fighting yeast infections and helping with joint problems and digestive problems. Kombucha helps bring your body back into balance so that it may heal itself naturally. The body is constantly striving to heal itself.

I have witnessed kombucha helping people with terrible coughs during cold and flu season and also with helping to prevent them. I would never have believed that kombucha was the powerful detoxifier if it had not happened to me. The first week that I started drinking kombucha I started to detoxify like crazy. Two things I noticed was how much I was going to the bathroom and I began to smell. The skin is the body's natural detoxifier and it was doing its job. My daughter had a similar experience. It only lasted a week and now I don't even need deodorant. Bad bacteria are the cause of body odor and I ingest so much good bacteria that I don't need deodorant anymore.

Besides all these benefits, it is the way it makes me feel that makes me love kombucha. It is a spirit lifter with all those B vitamins and amino acids. And then there is the fizz. It's true I am all about the fizz!

My Husband and Kombucha

My husband Ron is used to my crazy new ideas and has become accustomed to my enthusiasm for the latest discovery that I have made. So he goes along for the ride but never jumps in with both feet until coaxed. Kombucha was the first food he really grasped on to and here is why.

Ron was having trouble with his vision. He had a terrible problem with glare and driving at night. He finally went to an eye doctor and was diagnosed with cataracts. I didn't know this but there are different kinds of cataracts, and he had the kind that developed quickly, over a 6 month period and would have to have eye surgery. In the other eye another cataract was beginning and he would need surgery in probably the next three to 6 months. He was not happy. They don't know why it happens. "It just does" is what they said. He was only 40 and felt like he was 90. It was an awful feeling to be so young and need this surgery. Once again I knew his body was trying to tell us something. We needed to do something different, but what? He was not big yet on cultured foods; it scared him. When we first started making kombucha, my oldest daughter Maci told me to never ever let him look in the kombucha jar. If you have ever seen a Kombucha culture, you know what I am talking about. It is the weirdest looking thing. I have heard them called a brain, a placenta and a sludgy mass. Not sure that sludgy is a word but it fits. The kombucha culture is actually a combination of bacteria and yeast. It's really in the seaweed family, not a mushroom. I think it's beautiful.

I had done some research and read that kombucha was great for cataract prevention. So I told this to Ron and handed him a glass of my homemade kombucha. Much to my surprise he loved it. He started drinking it every day. I was super excited. He also started drinking kefir, as long as I made it into a smoothie for him.

Well, he had the surgery for the first eye. He was not a happy camper. But then something happened. They kept scheduling appointments because they said the other eye had the same fast growing cataract and within a few months he would need the surgery. But at every appointment they would check his eye and the doctor would sit back in his chair and say, "Huh, it stopped. What would make that cataract stop growing? I've never seen anything like that. Huh!" Fast forward 7 years and it is still the same. He's never had surgery in the other eye and is a faithful daily drinker of kombucha. Actually he loves the stuff.

I have no idea for sure what happened. Was it the kombucha? Was it the kefir? He drank kombucha more than anything else which led me to believe that it played a major part. Was his ecosystem changing inside and was it better able to get nutrients to his cells? I don't know for sure but I am thankful. I am thankful for the invisible world of microorganisms that have made themselves known to me.

How to make Kombucha

Time Required: 6-15 days

1. Wash all utensils with hot sudsy water and rinse well.

2. Boil three quarts of purified water.

3. Add 1 cup white sugar to water when a rolling boil is reached. Boil water and sugar for five minutes.

4. Turn off heat and add 4-5 tea bags of black or green tea.

5. Steep 10-15 minutes and remove tea leaves or bags and let tea cool (it doesn't hurt to steep the tea longer).

6. Pour cooled tea into gallon size glass container.

7. Add your Kombucha mushroom culture. Add 1 cup of fermented Kombucha Tea from a previous batch. You can add an extra cup of starter tea and your tea will ferment faster.

8. Place linen cloth over the opening of the jar and secure with a rubber band. This keeps dust, mold, spores and vinegar flies out of the fermenting tea.

9. Allow to sit undisturbed in a well ventilated and darkened place away from direct sunlight (65-90°F.) for 6 - 15 days.

10. To make sure the tea is ready to harvest; pour off a couple of ounces for a taste test.

11. Taste Test: A taste test on a batch of kombucha tea may taste like this: 4-6 Days - Too sweet, not all sugar converted. 7-9 Days - Tastes like sparkling apple cider. 10+ Days - Vinegar taste becoming prominent. It should taste tart and not sweet, but not overly sour.

12. When the tea is brewed to your taste, pour the tea into glass bottles and cap, then place in the refrigerator. This can now be second fermented with juices, but is delicious as it is.

13. Always leave enough starter tea from your last batch to make another batch of tea. You can remove the two cultures or leave them in the pot to make another batch. Make another pot of tea with sugar and add this to your starter and culture to start the process again.

Note: Sometimes the culture floats on the surface, sometimes it sinks to the bottom of the liquid. Either way is okay. When the culture sinks to the bottom a new culture (baby) will begin to grow on the surface of the tea.

Bubbly Fruit Flavored Kombucha

My daughter Maci and her fruit flavored fizzy kombucha. For those of you who don't want to spend the money to buy it, you can make it.

A friend of mine a couple of years ago was in a bad car accident. He actually broke the steering wheel off with his chest. He was in the hospital and was completely miserable on a gazillion pain killers and medications. His wife Paula, who is a good friend of mine, was talking to me about what hard a time he was having. I suggested she go buy some kombucha and bring it to him. It made him feel so much better that he went off all his pain killers and came home and started making kombucha himself. I had just learned how to make the fruit flavored kombucha and taught him how to make it. Now he makes the best fruit flavored kombucha I have ever had and he makes gallons of it each week. Kombucha is a powerful detoxifier and is loaded with B vitamins and it will lift your mood and just make you feel great. I just can't say enough about it.

You will need:

Kombucha that is already gone through the first ferment and is ready to drink.

100% fruit juice of your liking: I have used cherry, grape, blueberry pomegranate, lemon, pineapple, or a mixture of several juices.

Bottles that are designed for brewing. If you are using regular glass bottles you must beware, because kombucha can easily blow up your glass bottle if it has any flaws or the glass is too thin. My favorite bottles are the clamp down bottles by Grolsch (beer bottles). You can also find bottles at home brew stores. I get mine at www.brewcat.com.

The clamps down lids are safer and brewing bottles have a thick glass designed for brewing.

Take the brewed kombucha and place in clean sterilized bottles. You can strain the kombucha through a coffee filter to help prevent another kombucha culture forming but it is not necessary.

Add 1 to 2 ounces of fruit juice (per 12-14 ounces of kombucha) to your bottle and clamp shut. Leave a little room at the top of the bottle but not much. I use an electronic scale to measure the juice I put in. Label your bottles so you know when it started its second ferment.

Let your kombucha sit in a dark place for 1 to 3 weeks. Check after each week to see if the kombucha is bubbly enough for you. If not, let it ferment longer. Then place your bottles in the fridge to enjoy and slow down the fermenting. Be careful when opening bottles and never shake the bottle before opening!

Kombucha Iced Leche

Changing the world one drink at a time…

This drink has a super creamy frothy head on it. (It will also make you and the people at your party in a better mood!)

8 ounces of fruit flavored kombucha
3 ounces of milk
½ cup ice crushed
1 to 2 packages of Stevia or 1 tsp honey

Blend all in blender until super frothy about 30 seconds to 1 minute. Serve immediately and enjoy!

Maci's Citrus Syllabub

Delicious at the holidays.

¾ cup of Heavy Whipping Cream (I use raw milk cream and it's awesome)
½ lemon
½ orange
Little bit of Stevia or Sucanat
½ cup of Kombucha (Fruit flavored is best)

Measure Whipping Cream into a large mixing bowl and beat with a wire whisk or an electric mixer until it is thick. Set bowl aside. Juice the lemon and orange into a mixing bowl. Add the sweetener and Kombucha to the juice, stir until blended. Pour the juice mixture into the whipping cream stir (or fold) just enough to blend the juice and cream. The syllabub should be thick and frothy. (I chilled for 30 Minutes.) Serve in individual glasses.

Grape Kombucha Granita

Great in the summer time!

Pour one 16 oz bottle of grape Kombucha in an 8 X 8 pan. Add a handful of grapes. Put mixture in freezer. Within about 20 minutes, it should start to freeze. Don't walk away and forget it or you will have a solid block of ice. Break it up with a fork, and leave it in the freezer. Do this again in another 15 to 30 minutes or so. Keep this up until you have a pan of iced Kombucha slush. Place in a glass and enjoy.

Kombucha Floats Made With Kefir Ice Cream

One of my favorite discoveries was combining kefir and kombucha. Super frothy and bubbly!

4 to 8 ounces of your favorite kombucha
1 scoop of kefir ice cream (see page 18)

Pour 4 ounces of any flavor kombucha into a glass. Top with scoops of kefir ice cream. Add more kombucha if your glass has room. Be careful when adding ice cream that it doesn't over flow. It is foamy and bubbly.

Soooo good!!

Kombucha Raspberry Dressing & Strawberry Spinach Salad

¼ cup raspberry flavored kombucha
2 tsp Dijon mustard
2 Tbsp raspberry jam
2 tsp minced shallots
¾ cup olive oil
salt & pepper

Combine all ingredients except oil with wire whisk. Slowly pour oil while whisking to form emulsion. Refrigerate unused portion.

Spinach salad
Spinach, use amount according to guests
Handful of strawberries chopped
½ cup of pecans chopped
2 to 3 ounces of crumbled Gorgonzola cheese

Mix with all ingredients and top with dressing.

Sprouted Flour: the Answer to So Many Problems

I have met hundreds of people who are now on gluten free diets. My daughter used to be one of them. How can this grain that has been around since time began suddenly wreak such havoc on so many individuals? Well, it is definitely causing a lot of problems, but I was never one to just do something without understanding the reasoning behind it. I want to know the answers for myself and not just take someone's word for it. So when my daughter developed IBS (Irritable Bowel Syndrome), she couldn't eat wheat and every week the list kept getting bigger with things she couldn't tolerate. I became a woman on a mission to understand what was going on. One of the things I have always hated about modern medicine is that they slap a band aid on problems such as blood pressure, cholesterol and a host of other problems. My question is: why do you have high blood pressure and why can you suddenly not digest wheat and other foods? What causes the body to develop these symptoms? This is the best part of all our beautiful bodies. They call out to us with problems to get our attention. They are our best teachers and when you start having troubles. There is much to learn. The only way to learn is to go within and become attentive to something we take for granted: the inner world of our bodies. I will share with you what I learned. This is my journey to understanding and, while yours may be different, perhaps I can shed light on something that will help you.

Every morning my 16 year old daughter would climb out of bed and drag herself to the kitchen. Each morning I would pray that she would feel better that day. Her words were always the same. "I never feel good mom". It broke me. She was only 16 and she hated getting up every day to a life filled with pain. I took her to doctors and they wanted to remove her gallbladder for really no reason. It was just a guess. Then I took her to an acupuncturist. This was my first lesson in the body's ability to talk to you. With much kindness our Chinese acupuncturist talked with Maci. He said things to her like," You have too much hurry and worry and your body is hurting because of this." I remember as those words came out of his mouth and I fought back tears, because it was so true. She came home that afternoon and broke up with her boyfriend and then the journey really began. I started researching the foods that hurt her gut the most and eliminated them from her diet. The reason she was having so much trouble digesting grains was really twofold.

First, her gut lining was damaged. Stress and foods she was eating and a lack of nutrient dense foods was destroying her gut lining. Not enough of the right bacteria and enzymes to turn her foods into vitamins and fatty acids were causing much stress on her gut. There was nothing to protect her lining. Years of antibiotics had stripped her of all her good bacteria and left her defenseless. Just eliminating the food will eliminate the pain but then you need to fix the lining and add foods to do this. The best foods for this are cultured foods. She starting having a cultured food at every meal, kefir for breakfast and 1 to 2 Tbsp of cultured veggies at lunch and dinner, then kombucha or coconut kefir to drink at every meal. She also had a lot of bone broths made into soups. Bone broths are healing to the digestive track because of the collagen in the broth. She also ate a ton of coconut oil by the tablespoon, usually 3 tablespoons a day. I would watch as she got a burst of energy from this and was always amazed. All these foods are healing to the gut. Each one plays a different part in the healing.

Second, I discovered that grains are not the same as they used to be. For 100 of years they would cut the sheaths of grains and stack them in the fields and leave them to gather the next day. The dew would make the grains sprout and unlock the nutrients and deactivate the phytic acid and enzyme inhibitors. Then the workers would gather the grains and take the seeds off the stalks to be used. Today we have combine machine that take the seeds off instantly never allowing the grains to sprout. Then for years and still today in European countries we always used sourdough starters to raise our breads, which transform the bread in the same way that sprouting does. It puts lactobacillus into the bread and transforms the grain. These wonderful bacteria that not only change our breads into healthful foods also change our bodies the same way. Now we have instant yeasts that raise the breads quickly and the bread never has a chance to transform. Couple this with guts that are so damaged they can barely digest anything and you have a recipe for disaster. Grains take huge amounts of B vitamins to digest and when you are under a lot of stress you don't have what you need. Sprouting a grain activates all the B vitamins that are locked in the grain, and transforms the bread so you can digest it.

So here's the formula. Remove or deal with stress. Heal the gut with fermented foods and nutrient dense foods. Then once it is healed, add sprouted or sourdough grains. This is what I did and I have also watched many others do. My daughter can now eat anything and is free from a life sentence without grains. She loves life and can't wait to get out of bed. Food is not something that she is afraid of but something that brings her great joy. If you are reading this, chances are your body is trying to tell you something.

Your body is your best teacher; are you listening?

One of the other wonderful benefits is that sprouted grains are considered low glycemic. The pancreas needs huge amounts of B vitamins to deal with stress. Once a grain has been sprouted most bodies recognize it as a vegetable rather than a starch which requires vegetable enzymes not pancreatic enzymes. Therefore, eating sprouted grains does not stress the pancreas. This is great for diabetics.

You can buy sprouted bread at any health food store. I love sprouting and making my own flour. It takes a little equipment but I sprout 13 lbs at a time and the flour will last 6 months stored at room temperature, or longer in the refrigerator. I love taking grains and turning them into bread. You can use the flour just like you would in any recipe. It is worth the investment it has been life changing for me and my family.

Happy and successful cooking doesn't rely only on know-how; it comes from the heart, makes great demands on the palate and needs enthusiasm and a deep love of food to bring it to life.
Georges Blanc, 'Ma Cuisine des Saisons'

How to Make Sprouted Flour

Place wheat berries in a bowl. Cover them with filtered water for 36 hours with at least 1 inche of water above the grains. They will get tiny little tails and be a little bubbly. Rinse them in warm water and drain. Place them in dehydrator at 100°F for 8 to 10 hours or until dry and crunchy. Then grind in a grain mill for flour. This flour will last 6 months on the counter. For longer storage, place flour in refrigerator or freezer. Do not over sprout them. The tails should be very tiny. You have to look closely to see the little white tips coming out of the wheat berry. This is the perfect amount of sprouting and insures the most nutrients and best tasting bread.

Sprouted Whole Wheat Bread

This is the bread I make most often. Great for sandwiches.

Makes 1 loaf

1- ½ cups water
¼ cup olive oil
¼ cup honey
2 ¼ tsp dry yeast
2 tsp Celtic sea salt
3 to 5 cups sprouted whole-wheat flour

Add ingredients in order to kitchen aid bowl. Process dough until it pulls away from the bowl and forms a ball of dough, if you have a mixer. Place in a greased bowl and let rise until double, about an hour. Punch down and form into loaf and place in greased loaf pan. Let rise again until double about an hour. Bake at 375°F for 30 to 35 minutes.

Kayli's Cinnamon Swirl Bread

I have never met a 13 year old girl who has impressed me more than Kayli. I am proud to call her my friend and helper in making this book. She has more wisdom than most women twice her age. The special way she designed the bread so that the cinnamon spirals in the middle is genius. Thanks, Kayli, I can't wait to see what you will do next.

3 Tbsp of cinnamon
4-5 Tbsp of coconut sugar or sucanat

Use the Sprouted Whole Wheat Bread recipe on previous page to make dough.

After mixing, place dough in oiled bowl and allow to rise until doubled in size (about an hour). Place dough on oiled surface and shape into a rectangle about 20 inches long and 6 inches wide. The dough should be about ½ inch thick.

Spread cinnamon evenly over the rectangle and then the sugar. Starting at one end, tightly roll the dough towards the center stopping at the middle. Then roll the other side towards the middle. Both sides will be rolled together to form the loaf. Gently pinch the seam together. Place in greased loaf pan with seam side down.

Let rise for about an hour. Bake at 375°F for 35 minutes. Allow to cool before slicing.

Sprouted Pizza Dough

If you want to add more flavor, replace the olive oil with a basil olive oil or a garlic flavored one.

For the dough:
1 ¼ cups warm (100 to 110 F) water
2 packages dry yeast
1 tablespoon honey
2 tsp salt
3 Tbsp olive oil
4 cups sprouted whole wheat flour, plus extra for kneading

Directions:

Mix the dough. Combine the water, yeast, honey and 3 tablespoons of olive oil in the bowl of an electric mixer fitted with a dough hook. When the yeast is dissolved, add 3 cups of flour, then 2 teaspoons salt, and mix on medium-low speed. While mixing, add up to 1 more cup of flour, or just enough to make a soft dough. Knead the dough for about 10 minutes until smooth, sprinkling it with the flour as necessary to keep it from sticking to the bowl. Place the dough in a well-oiled bowl and turn it to cover it lightly with oil. Cover the bowl with a kitchen towel and allow the dough to rise at room temperature for 30 minutes.

Preheat oven to 500°F. Divide dough into 3 balls and work with one and place the others in the bowl. Roll out each ball and stretch until desired shape. Place on pizza pan and add toppings. Bake for 10 to 15 minutes, until the crusts are crisp and the cheeses begin to brown. Watch closely!

Nancy's Hamburger Buns

This recipe is from my friend Nancy, who sat across from me one afternoon and told me that I had to write this book. Feeling very uncertain and hesitant she convinced me that what I had learned needed to be shared. She has inspired me to be more than I ever thought I could be. She is an up lifter and a light that shines the way for others to follow. My heart is most grateful to know such a soul as Nancy. Try her wheat buns. I am pretty sure they will be the best you have ever had. Nancy always does things to perfection.

Yield: 12 buns
1 ½ cups water
4 Tbsp maple syrup
4 Tbsp gently melted butter
2 tsp yeast
1 ½ tsp salt
4 cups sprouted whole wheat flour

Add ingredients in order into mixer using dough hook. Allow mixer to knead dough until dough ball looks smooth. Dough should be soft and wet, not forming a hard ball. The softer the dough, the softer the buns. If you add too much flour, the buns will turn out too dense. Let rise until doubled in oiled bowl. Then divide the dough ball into 12 equal sized balls. Placed in oiled muffin top pan. Let rise again for at least 45 minutes. Bake at 375°F for 11 minutes. Do not over bake for the softest results.

There is no sight on earth more appealing than the sight of a woman making dinner for someone she loves.
Thomas Wolfe (1900-1938)

Sprouted Graham Crackers

You can use these to make graham cracker pie crusts. Place these crackers in a food processor and pulse until they turn into a finely ground meal.

2 cups sprouted wheat flour
¼ tsp salt
¼ tsp baking soda
⅛ tsp baking powder
4 Tbsp honey
5 Tbsp butter melted
2 to 4 Tbsp water Add to make a ball that is not sticking to touch

Mix all dry ingredients. Add butter and water until ball is formed. Roll out onto buttered or parchment lined baking sheet using a rolling pin. With a knife score into 16 crackers and prick with a fork. Bake at 350 for 20 to 25 minutes. Use the longer time for crisper graham crackers. You can grind these in a food processor to make graham cracker crumbs.

Sprouted Tortillas

Super easy to make and fun for kids who like to help. These also freeze very well.

Yields: 10

2 cups sprouted whole wheat flour or spelt flour
½ tsp salt
3 tbsp olive oil
⅔ cup warm water

Combine flour and salt in a bowl or food processor, add the oil and mix thoroughly. Mix the water while the food processor is running. Let the dough sit for 10 minutes covered. Turn out the dough onto a lightly floured surface, knead it a couple times and pat into a disk. Pull and roll the pieces into 10 to 12 pieces. If you have a tortilla press (I highly recommend them; they are cheap and super handy) use it to flatten each ball as you make and cook them. If you're rolling by hand, take one of the balls and flatten it into a small disk. Using a floured rolling pin and a floured surface, roll the tortilla into a flat disk about 6- to 8 inches in diameter. Heat a heavy ungreased griddle over medium high heat. Toss tortilla onto griddle and let it heat for 1 minute the use tongs and flip to bake on other side. Bake until each side begins to brown and puff in spots, about 1 minute per side. While the first tortilla is cooking, roll the next one. Transfer the baked tortilla to a plate and make the next one. Cover them with a towel to keep them soft and warm.

Strawberry Scones with Probiotic Topping

My daughter Maci had some girlfriends over one night, and I made this for breakfast the next morning. It was a hit and became one of our favorites. It is even better left over the next day. The strawberries make this super moist and the lemon topping enhances the taste of the strawberries.

Yields: 8

2 cups sprouted flour
⅓ cup sucanat
2 teaspoon baking powder
¼ teaspoon salt
⅓ cup chilled butter, cut into pieces
1 egg
⅔ cups cream or milk
1 teaspoon vanilla extract
1 cup chopped strawberries
Egg wash, 1 egg and 1 teaspoon water, beaten

Lemon Topping
16 oz Greek yogurt
1 tbsp kefir
¼ lemon zest and juice
2 package Stevia or 2 tsp of honey

Preheat oven: 325°F. *Optional scone pan read note.*

Combine flour, sugar, baking powder and salt. Cut in butter with pastry blender. Combine wet ingredients and mix into dry just until moistened. Add strawberries. Mixture will be very sticky. Turn onto floured surface and knead 4 to 5 times with floured hands. Pat out to 1/2-inch thick and cut circles. Brush tops with egg wash. Sprinkle tops with sugar and sliced almonds. Place on greased baking sheet. Bake for 25 to 30 minutes.

Topping
Mix yogurt and kefir. Squeeze lemon into yogurt, zest lemon and add to yogurt, stir in sweetener. Scoop onto scone.

* If you have a scone pan you can just scoop it into the pan and bake. No kneading or flouring required.

Question and Answers about Kefir

Can I make almond or coconut milk Kefir, and is the process the same?

If you use the milk grains for culturing almond or coconut milk you need to refresh them occasionally with dairy milk. This can be as simple as leaving them 24 hours in a half-cup of milk, then straining them.

Why is my kefir starting to separate and curdle?

This means that it is culturing faster. One cause is that your grains have grown and this will make it culture faster. You can remove some of the grains or add more milk next time so the grain to milk ratio has been increased. It can also mean that your kitchen is warmer and this can also make it culture faster. You can shorten the time it cultures so that it does not separate as fast. It is not a bad thing if it separates. This just means it is done and you can shake or stir the kefir to mix it together again after you remove the grains.

I left my Kefir grains in the refrigerator for a few months. Are they still good?

Probably not. Kefir grains eat the milk sugars or lactose out of the milk and make their bacteria. This is why the milk is sourer. When they run out of food they begin to die. They are living organisms and need food to live and produce their beneficial bacteria. Treat them like a pet and make sure you feed them.

I stored my kefir grains in the fridge for a week. Is the milk the grains are in ok to drink?

The milk that the grains are in is not really kefir. It would not hurt you to drink it, but it probably won't taste very good. Kefir needs to culture at a warmer temperature to really be kefir.

Do I culture kefir with a lid or with cheese cloth?

I always culture my kefir with a lid on. I use a quart glass canning jar with a plastic lid. You can also use a metal jar lid.

Why aren't my grains growing?

If you are making kefir everyday your grains should be growing and multiplying. If they are not it is because the temperature in your house is colder and this will slow them down, or your grains have died. If your milk is turning into kefir by becoming sour and thick your grains are still working just growing at a slower rate. You can always purchase more or get some new grains from a friend.

How do I know if my grains are still good?

They will culture your milk and turn it sour and thick within 24 to 48 hours. Make sure that you have enough grains for the amount of milk that you are using. 1 to 2 tablespoons per cup of milk.

Questions and Answers about Cultured Vegetables

How long do I culture my vegetables on the counter? Can I go longer?

To do most vegetables, it takes 6 days at room temperature. There are a few that only take 3 days but they are stated in the recipe. If you culture them longer than 6 days they can get too yeasty and the flavor will change and not taste as well. They continue to ferment after you place them in the fridge, but at a slower rate and the flavors develop and age like a fine wine that is delicious!

Do I have to put a culture in the veggies to make cultured veggies?

I have made sauerkraut without a veggie culture or whey and they turned out delicious. I would recommend cultures for other culture veggies because it seems to insure that you will have a consistent product. It also adds more good bacteria to the veggies giving you more probiotics.

How long will my cultured veggies last?

In the refrigerator cultured veggies will last at least 9 months or longer. The will age much the same a fine wine ages. Many of my vegetables taste better at 6 and 8 weeks in the fridge. It is fun to taste them at different stages along the way.

Why aren't my vegetables crunchy?

Salt is the key to this. Vegetables without salt become soft and slimy. Vegetables made with salt will produce a crunchy vegetable.

Can these foods be stored out of the fridge after they have been fermented?

Technically they can be stored in a cooler basement or cold cellar. However they continue to ferment and don't taste very good. They do best and taste best at colder temperatures such as when being stored in a refrigerator. Remember when proper lacto-fermentation has occurred then, you cannot get sick! The good bacteria are dominating and cannot let other harmful bacteria in.

How will I know if my vegetables are properly fermented?

They will taste sour and look bubbly. If your vegetables have an off smell, you will know this by the strong odor that will smell unappetizing. Cultured veggies taste sour and delicious.

What are the white spots on my veggies?

This is harmless mold. If the vegetables climb up above the water they will mold. You scrape off the mold and submerge vegetables under water. Check from time to time while they are fermenting to make sure they stay submerged under the water.

Questions and Answers about Kombucha

Why did my mushroom sink to the bottom? Is it ok?

When you make your first batch of kombucha your mushroom will most likely sink or float. You will get a new mother that will grow on top of your tea each time you make a new batch of kombucha. This will not affect the brew or taste of your kombucha and is perfectly fine.

My kombucha is still sweet what did I do wrong?

Your house is probably colder and it takes longer to ferment in colder temperatures. I use a brew belt which you can find on my site under, "Things I use". You can also use a heating pad but brew belts work the best. Let it ferment longer and the sweetness will be eaten by the yeasts and bacteria.

There is mold on my mushroom, is it still safe to consume the tea?

No, it's not safe! There can be a couple things going on here. Many people do not put it in the right ratios of sugar and tea to starter culture and the teas don't ferment properly. The other cause can be air born molds in the house. I have had a few people develop this after that had a leaky roof or placed their pot in a closet that did not circulate enough air and then developed mold. Once mold has developed, it is very important to toss the whole batch--including the kombucha scoby and tea. Then purchase a new starter culture or find a friend who can share one.

Can I cut up my kombucha mushroom?

Yes absolutely. You only need a part of the mushroom to ferment. You can even make a pot of kombucha without the mushroom and use just the starter tea. It will take up to 3 weeks but it can still be done.

How do I increase the carbonation of my kombucha tea?

Second fermenting is the best way to achieve this. It needs the extra sugars and the juice in the capped off bottle for the yeast to turn the sugars into natural carbonation. See my section on how to make bubbly fruit flavored kombucha.

What type of tea should I use to make kombucha?

Black tea or green tea or a combination of both is the preferred method. But you can use almost any type of tea. White, jasmine or rooibos teas can all be used. I would not recommend herbal teas or fruit flavored teas with oils many of them contain anti bacteria qualities that could affect the outcome of your tea.

About The Author

DONNA SCHWENK is the Kansas City Chapter leader for the Weston Price Foundation, a worldwide organization comprised of people dedicated to restoring nutrient dense food to the human diet through education research and activism. She is continually teaching classes in the Kansas City area, to teach others what she has learned. She has been making and eating cultured foods since 2002. The dramatic change in her health and that of her family has given her a sense of well being that has been incredible. After years of research, life experience, and teaching classes to help others, it is her pleasure to share it with you.

Resources, Links and Books

My website and blog; http://culturedfoodlife.com/

http://blog.culturedfoodlife.com/

I am the Kansas City chapter leader for the Weston Price Foundation, a nonprofit organization that helps people find healthy and life giving foods. http://www.westonaprice.org/

This is a great place to purchase your starters for kefir and kombucha and veggies, and many others wonderful ferments. http://www.culturesforhealth.com/

Donna Gates and the Body Ecology diet are a great resource for education and resources in learning about cultured foods. http://bodyecology.com/index.php

Sandor Katz was the first class I went to on fermentation. There is much to learn from this man and his books. The guru of fermentation, I find him brilliant. http://www.wildfermentation.com/

Books

One of the books that changed my life many years ago. If you only buy one book, buy this one. Nourishing Traditions: The Cookbook that Challenges Politically Correct Nutrition and the Diet Dictocrats By Sally Fallon

Wild Fermentation: The Flavor, Nutrition, and Craft of Live-Culture Foods
By Sandor Ellix Katz

Great book with a few recipes on cultured foods. Full Moon Feast: Food and the Hunger for Connection by Jessica Prentice

Healed from Crones disease, Jordan used cultured foods to heal his body.
The Maker's Diet by Jordan Rubin

This book has a lot of easy recipes using sprouted flour and nutrient dense foods.
The Diet Rebels Cookbook: Eating Clean and Green
By Jillayne Clements, Michelle Stewart

This is the woman who opened my eyes to the benefits of using and making sprouted flour. Essential Eating Sprouted Baking
By Janie Quinn

Traditional Foods Are Your Best Medicine: Improving Health and Longevity with Native Nutrition
By Ronald F. Schmid N.D.

Truly Cultured: Rejuvenating Taste, Health and Community With Naturally Fermented Foods
by Nancy Lee Bentley

These next two books were written from a physician who has walk the walk and talks the talk.

Gut and Psychology Syndrome: Natural Treatment for Dyspraxia, Autism, ADD, Dyslexia, ADHD, Depression, Schizophrenia. By Dr. Natasha Campbell-McBride MD

Put Your Heart in Your Mouth
by Dr Natasha Campbell-McBride

The Untold Story of Milk: The History, Politics and Science of Nature's Perfect Food: Raw Milk from Pasture-Fed Cows: By Ron Schmid

Wonderful recipes for kefir and yogurt, and the benefits of including them in your diet.
The Yogurt Diet: By Ana Luque

The Raw Milk Revolution: Behind America's Emerging Battle Over Food Rights
By David E. Gumpert

Real Food for Mother and Baby: Nina Planck

The Grassfed Gourmet Cookbook: Healthy Cooking & Good Living with Pasture Raised Foods
by Shannon Hayes

Eat Fat, Lose Fat: The Healthy Alternative to Trans Fats
By Mary Enig, Sally Fallon

Nutrition and Physical Degeneration
by Weston A. Price

I use the book constantly. This is a wonderful resource for home cheese making.
Home Cheese Making: Recipes for 75 Delicious Cheeses
By Ricki Carroll

Know Your Fats: The Complete Primer for Understanding the Nutrition of Fats, Oils and Cholesterol
By Mary G. Enig

Performance without Pain: A Step-by-Step Nutritional Program for Healing Pain, Inflammation and Chronic Ailments in Musicians, Athletes, Dancers . . . and Everyone Else
By Kathryne Pirtle

Made in the USA
Lexington, KY
17 May 2012